THE
5-MINUTE
TEACHER

*How do I maximize time for
learning in my classroom?*

Mark
BARNES

 Alexandria, VA USA

arias™

Website: www.ascd.org   www.ascdarias.org
E-mail: books@ascd.org

Printed in the United States of America. Cover art © 2013 by ASCD. ASCD publications present a variety of viewpoints. The views expressed or implied in this book should not be interpreted as official positions of the Association.

ASCD LEARN TEACH LEAD® and ASCD ARIAS™ are trademarks owned by ASCD and may not be used without permission. All referenced trademarks are the property of their respective owners.

PAPERBACK ISBN: 978-1-4166-1708-2   ASCD product #SF113072
Also available as an e-book (see Books in Print for the ISBNs).

Library of Congress Cataloging-in-Publication Data
Barnes, Mark.
  The 5-minute teacher : how do I maximize time for learning in my classroom? / Mark Barnes.
      pages cm
  Includes bibliographical references.
  ISBN 978-1-4166-1708-2 (pbk. : alk. paper) 1. Student-centered learning. 2. Effective teaching. 3. Classroom management. I. Title. II. Title: Five-minute teacher.
  LB1027.23.B368 2013
  370.15'4—dc23
                                2013020764

21 20 19 18 17 16 15 14 13   1 2 3 4 5 6 7 8 9 10

THE 5-MINUTE TEACHER

How do I maximize time for learning in my classroom?

Want to earn a free ASCD Arias e-book?
Your opinion counts! Please take 2–3 minutes to give
us your feedback on this publication. All survey
respondents will be entered into a drawing to
win an ASCD Arias e-book.

Click here or type in this web location:
www.ascd.org/ariasfeedback

Thank you!

Introduction

It was the end of class. Twenty-five students—seated around tables, in beanbag chairs, and at computers—brought an end to nearly as many activities. A smiling young man shook his head and called out, "Mr. Barnes, this class goes by so fast. My other classes are so slow."

I shrugged, smiled inwardly, and replied (somewhat stereotypically), "Well, time flies when you're having fun." There is no magic behind making each 55-minute class enjoyable for my students. I've learned that the hard way. It's the structure of the student-centered classroom that creates a powerful, exciting learning environment that students actually *enjoy*. The so-called five-minute teacher—who should be nearly invisible—is just part of the fun.

Five minutes. Three hundred seconds. It can be like a whisper disappearing in an instant, or it can feel like an eternity—depending on the content that fills the time. Still, five minutes can be the most important part of a student's day. When students are poised to learn something new, five minutes can prepare them for experiences that will open doors and minds. The trick is making those five minutes count.

In more than 20 years as a classroom teacher, I've learned that 45–55 minutes can be a complete waste of time, whereas a few well-planned, well-executed seconds can create remarkable new learning opportunities. Highly motivated students may be better equipped to listen to lengthy lectures and 30-minute lessons, but they'll learn the material equally well, and perhaps better, if they investigate the content after instruction that lasts five minutes or less. Reluctant learners are prone to become disruptive as soon as a lesson surpasses the 300-second mark. In fact, you'll probably lose them much faster if you don't engage them immediately.

What if any teacher could improve learning and change lives while teaching less? Notwithstanding the Common Core State Standards, high-stakes testing, Student Learning Objectives, or any other constraints that make teachers believe they must spend countless hours creating lengthy lesson plans, it's time for educators to move toward doing less. I don't mean to suggest that teachers should put *less effort* into planning and executing their lessons. Rather, I'm referring to a shift in philosophy—one that's about valuing every minute of every class and making those minutes look and feel different from how they currently look and feel. In the following pages, we'll explore a different vision of teaching and learning, and, hopefully, you'll discover the power of becoming a five-minute teacher and building a student-centered classroom.

Quickly Identify What's Most Important

I recognize that the term *five-minute teacher* might imply direct instruction that only lasts for five minutes. In other words, five minutes of teaching followed by student work for the remaining time. Although some days might look like this (depending on the activity or project), the term actually refers to the idea that the teacher should never stand and deliver content for more than five minutes at a stretch. Instead, instruction should occur in brief increments, allowing students to explore content independently and collaboratively and to use rich project-based activities, collaborative conversations, mobile devices, and digital tools.

A five-minute teacher works much harder than an "old-school," stand-and-deliver teacher who lectures for 15–25 minutes before relegating students to some mundane, rote-memory practice activity. When you become a five-minute teacher, you craft brief lessons that weave their way seamlessly through student-centered, inquiry-based discussions, activities, and projects. A five-minute teacher is the perfect combination of artist, entertainer, leader, follower, and magician—a master educator who isn't afraid to get out of students' way so they can discover learning with little guidance.

For those who are comfortable with the traditional stand-and-deliver model, this concept may seem abstract or incomprehensible. Even the average progressive-minded teacher who integrates technology and collaboration may use 15 or more minutes for direct instruction. If you teach long blocks—say 70–90 minutes—you might honestly need 15 or more minutes of what looks like direct instruction. A five-minute teacher, though, will break these 15 minutes into three or more segments and use video, questioning, collaboration, reflection, and other innovative means to create a class with plenty of forward motion and effective transitions from teacher-directed time to student-directed time. Although these concepts are not new, understanding how to use them efficiently is critical for a successful five-minute teacher.

Excellent student-centered lessons eliminate many of the traditional activities that bore students and diminish learning. Therefore, understanding what to keep and what to throw away each day is essential. The following sample lesson illustrates how traditional activities and lectures are replaced with engaging, progressive practices that help students soak up information and become independent learners. This approach is outlined in more detail in my book, *Role Reversal: Achieving Uncommonly Excellent Results in the Student-Centered Classroom* (2013).

To visualize effective instruction in five minutes or less, imagine a middle school history teacher who works in 60-minute blocks. She is introducing a lesson on the Civil War that might typically need 15–20 minutes of instruction. This instruction includes assistance from various supplemental materials, such as slides, textbooks, or handouts that contain information about events that sparked the war. After a boring, rote-memory activity, the teacher asks some whole-group questions, which only a handful of students hear and to which even fewer respond. Regardless of what students are doing that might appear to be interactive on the surface (e.g., copying notes or answering textbook questions), this is ultimately teacher-led, unimaginative direct instruction that will, in most instances, detract from real learning.

With this in mind, what strategies and tools might a creative five-minute teacher employ? First, let's consider how she might deliver instruction for this same Civil War lesson. Whereas the traditional teacher instructs students to copy causes of the war from the whiteboard, the five-minute teacher begins the class by dividing students into two groups—the North and the South. (This kind of role-play can be applied to almost any class.) The activity begins when a student is told that she represents South Carolina and is starting a sort of mutiny called a secession. She wants to leave the other states because she doesn't want the same things that they want. Soon, more students secede, and sides are drawn for a simulated war.

Carefully written instructions that explain the simulation are delivered. The instructions—which can be posted on a whiteboard, classroom website, blog, or sheet of paper—direct students to divide each of the groups into three subgroups, representing regiments that will fight different battles. Maps are provided (either via web links or on paper), and students are directed to plan their offense or defense. Note that, unlike a traditional lesson, this five-minute teacher activity does not begin with events that led to the Civil War. The simulation engages students in collaboration, planning, and problem solving. This initial enthusiasm sparks further curiosity about the actual events. The initial simulation lasts approximately 15 minutes, and the instruction for the division of sides and ensuing contest might take a total of three or four minutes.

A whole-group discussion follows the small-group simulation, and students share the plans they made for attack and defense. Tapping into her student-centered resource toolkit, the teacher encourages the use of Twitter to make this Q&A segment even more engaging. She encourages students to tweet their questions and comments with a designated hashtag (such as #warsim, for *war simulation*, in this example). She then displays the "conversation" on the interactive whiteboard, and all tweets that include the relevant hashtag are projected to the whole class. The goal of the five-minute teacher is for 100 percent participation in all activities, and online conversation greatly facilitates this. Students are usually excited to be part of this kind of discussion. Indeed, Twitter is one of the most powerful communication platforms available, and it's one teachers rarely consider for classroom use.

The idea here is to throw away the rote-memorization activities that many teachers use to begin a unit—completing workbook pages, copying notes, or outlining a textbook chapter. These methods should be replaced with exciting, often abstract, discovery activities that place the responsibilities for thinking and creativity squarely on each learner.

At this point in the lesson—maybe 25 to 30 minutes into class—the teacher shares an engaging video excerpt that highlights the causes of the Civil War and sparks curiosity among students. This is followed by small-group collaboration and student-generated questions. A five-minute teacher offers limited guidance here, as it's important for students to ignite the discussion on their own. She might offer one example to start the discussion and then ask students to continue with their own. One obvious example is "Why did South Carolina secede from the Union?" From there, the teacher circulates, listening to conversations and encouraging higher-level thinking and questioning. She might tell a struggling group to use "What if?" questions, providing examples if necessary. This questioning technique is a powerful tool in the student-centered classroom that will be discussed in more detail later.

Once students create questions within their small groups, they share them in a variety of ways—on butcher paper; in a blog; or with another tool, such as TodaysMeet, which creates private online discussions that are similar to hashtag-linked Twitter conversations. This sparks further productive discussion. Although the teacher adds a few inquiries of her own, the students' questions drive the learning. Again, acting in her capacity as five-minute teacher, she ensures participation from all students, quiets those who may want to dominate, and helps focus the discussion on the topic at hand. Typically, though, enough information has been provided in the simulation, video, and small-group discussion for learning outcomes to be met.

The class ends with a written reflection on what was learned. Students could respond to a guiding question that was asked at the beginning of class, or they could summarize the class discussion and what they learned about the topic as a result. This can be done in a journal or blog post, and the task requires 5–10 minutes, depending on the individual student. The specific method for how students reflect doesn't matter; the process of reflection is an essential part of internalizing learning. "Reflection thus forms the important link between processing the new information and integrating it with the existing understanding of the world around" (Ong, 2004, p. 3). It's this real-world connection that engages students who might otherwise have very little interest in what they assume to be a "boring" academic topic such as the Civil War.

The key to any lesson's success is self-discovery. Although the traditional teaching model is built on sharing the relevant objective or standard and exactly what students will learn, the five-minute teacher encourages students to discover concepts and skills on their own. Using some sort of guiding question is certainly an acceptable (if not preferred) way to begin a class, but telling students exactly what they'll learn is both presumptuous and poor practice. Asking a guiding question such as "Why did the United States break apart and ultimately fight our country's bloodiest war?" is a thought-provoking way to focus students on the day's lesson before they engage in a role-play. This is the kind of question that sparks discussion and debate and raises more questions; it is an essential question (McTighe & Wiggins, 2013).

The simulated battle planning and brief video are fun for students, but they also promote curiosity. Students receive just enough information to create guiding questions on their own, and when they ask one another questions, they are much more invested in the answers than they might have been if the teacher had posed all of the questions. In other words, students feel a sense of freedom as they engage with the material and one another; they're not simply responding to a teacher's control, which discourages learning. As I've pointed out elsewhere, "letting go of control may be the single most important part of creating a successful classroom" (Barnes, 2013, p. 11). If you've never used this sort of inquiry-based approach to learning, then you'll be amazed at how much information students acquire when they have the opportunity to ask the questions.

Another tool five-minute teachers use is video—perhaps the most powerful medium for hooking student attention to a subject. I'll discuss video in a later section, so, for now, let's focus on aspects of video use that make it effective in the classroom. Chief among them is brevity. One to four minutes should be the guideline, depending on how much discussion is required to support the video and explain it in context.

Using movies is acceptable for launching some activities, but it's important to think carefully and choose wisely which segments you will show. Breaking up a movie and showing segments over several brief lessons in one class is an effective use of video instruction. For example, I have used the 1983 movie version of *The Outsiders* to launch a unit on S. E. Hinton's young adult novel. Prior to students reading the book, I'll show the scene where the two gangs—the Greasers and the Socs—rumble. Without knowing anything about the book, students are immediately compelled by a story that involves this kind of action and conflict. Later in the same class, I'll show another excerpt from the movie that sparks debate about one of the novel's most important themes. For example, the scene in which Johnny remembers that Ponyboy likes the novel *Gone With the Wind* and surprises him with a copy is one of many scenes that demonstrate the value of friendship. This method engages students and creates genuine, inherent interest in the material, whereas a more routine activity—such as copying notes about 1960s gang life—will most likely turn them off.

Allow Students to Teach Themselves

The most difficult part of becoming a five-minute teacher is knowing when to stop talking, which is truly an art. When I converted my traditional classroom to a Results Only Learning Environment, I realized that talking less was essential to the success of a progressive, student-centered classroom (Barnes, 2013). As long as I was talking, the students weren't, and that ultimately led to them becoming disconnected from the material. Talking less became so important to me, in fact, that I once used a timer to ensure that I only talked for about three minutes during any part of class. However, this is not a practice I would recommend. Using a timer became too cumbersome and intrusive, and I stopped using one as soon as I became accustomed to limiting my direct instruction to a few minutes. The more natural and "organic" your instruction feels to students, the more they'll respond to it.

Initially, talking less was difficult for me. I was concerned about all of the information that I had to deliver during each class. Indeed, teachers must, on a daily basis, face thick curriculum guides, countless standards, and pressure from administrators to help students pass high-stakes tests. Unfortunately, this often results in cramming backpacks full of material into short increments of time, which in turn leads to long lectures and prolonged seatwork. I've found that even five to eight minutes of direct instruction, bereft of any interruptions, is far too much. This is the guiding principle of the five-minute teacher.

Although it took me many years to learn, I eventually realized that I could break up my direct instruction into brief, well-placed segments throughout a given class. This may sound easy, but it can be quite challenging for even the most adroit orators. You need to keep reminding yourself that when students use discovery activities, they begin teaching one another. Therefore, when teaching *The Outsiders*, I might show two to three minutes of the movie, followed by two minutes of comments or questions. Before I embraced the tenets of the five-minute teacher, I would often spend eight to ten minutes on the prereading points I wanted to make about social class discrimination, decision making, friendship, and loyalty. Now, if the class is structured properly, my students will flesh out many of these concepts for themselves through discovery learning. Direct instruction that explicitly identifies the concepts is unnecessary.

After the rumble scene, I stop the movie and ask, "Based on this scene, what do you think this book is about? Let's write three ideas in our journals." This introductory lesson, including the video excerpt and instruction for writing, takes about four minutes. I've still got plenty to add, but I'll get to it after the students write independently and then share their thoughts with one another. This is far more efficient and engaging than having students copy notes about the novel and its author.

On the first day of a unit about *The Outsiders*, I want students to understand that we'll explore various crucial life decisions that young people make. A traditional teacher would likely include these points in a lengthy lecture. By contrast, a five-minute teacher should encourage students to participate in a group discussion and unravel the importance of decision making for young adults. For example, after students watch a scene from the movie in which one boy kills a rival gang member, they'll write their opinions of how this scene might affect the story's plot. This decision affects the characters' lives for the remainder of the story, but it's important not to give this information away. Let students arrive at this realization by themselves.

When faced with this type of writing activity, many students will write exactly what their teacher wants them to learn (if they know it). However, in the absence of such specific guidance, students are forced to express their own thoughts and feelings. When they share their writing with peers, the teacher should emphasize the most on-point observations by mentioning particular examples to the whole group. For example, "Aaron makes a fascinating point when he writes that killing the rival gang member will affect Johnny and Ponyboy's decision about what to do next." Other students then have the freedom to agree (or disagree, as the case may be) and add their own opinions. A five-minute teacher understands that peers' words can carry a lot more weight than his or her own, and there is nothing wrong with students doing the teaching.

Plan to the Minute

Teachers are taught in their preservice years to plan their lessons carefully—write a goal and objective, list materials and procedures, and summarize closure. This is not an entirely obsolete way to create a lesson plan, but a five-minute teacher needs something much more precise. The following model is a good template and can be refined to fit your own comfort level and immediate needs.

Guiding question: Why did the United States break apart and ultimately fight our country's bloodiest war?

1. Direction (3–5 minutes): Give instructions for creating a North versus South simulation. Open with "Today, we're going to start a war." Provide instructions for how the two groups will plan a simulated battle. Distribute a handout with step-by-step guidelines for mapping out attacks and defense perimeters. Provide battle maps for all groups.

2. Collaboration (12–15 minutes): Following specific written directions, the two groups create subgroups and coordinate their plans. Circulate from one group to the next, listening, commenting, and helping when needed.

3. Whole-group Q&A (5 minutes): Based on the simulation, students answer one or two questions posed by the teacher and other students, and they discuss their observations about the simulated battle plans. Use Twitter to conduct this conversation. Be sure students know how to use the hashtag you create.

4. Video presentation (1–3 minutes): Show the first minute or so of an educational video about the causes of the Civil War, bringing class discussion into focus.

5. Small-group inquiry (6–8 minutes): Have each small group create at least one question and one observation about the Civil War and its causes, based on what the group has learned so far. These should be written on butcher paper.

6. Sharing (4–5 minutes): Groups post their questions and observations in a common space for all to see. They should also assign a representative to share these with the class.

7. Reflection (8–10 minutes): Students write what they've learned in the class, focusing on their understanding of the Civil War and its causes. (Give the option to write on a class or personal blog or in a journal.)

Notice that not every minute of the class period is planned. This allows for transitions from one activity to the next and for a cushion to any part that runs long. In a student-centered classroom that is orchestrated by a master five-minute teacher, some segments run beyond their planned time because of intense student engagement or intelligent discourse. This should always be looked upon as a positive, and having a few extra minutes built in makes for smart planning.

Harness the Power of Video

Years ago, I introduced my class website (www.barnesclass.com), which soon became a hub for my classes and a go-to resource for the entire school year. Although I had previously used video to augment lessons, the process was often more troublesome than helpful, requiring precious teaching and learning minutes to locate the desired video or have students type in extraordinarily long web addresses. The classroom website eliminated these hurdles and made video presentation a seamless support tool. The site serves as a dynamic repository of content that students can revisit at any time. Without obstacles impeding its efficiency, video should be an integral piece of daily instruction and a pivotal tool for the five-minute teacher.

Recall previous lesson examples about the Civil War and *The Outsiders*. Both of these contained video supplements to direct instruction. A one- or two-minute video (from sources such as YouTube, TeacherTube, Vimeo, TED-Ed, Discovery Educator Network, and CNN) is easily embedded on a classroom website and can be quickly accessed by both teacher and student. The right videos can serve as invaluable springboards into student-centered learning activities, and they can prompt thought-provoking lesson starters or assets for further enrichment.

Although there are countless resources that contain material teachers can place on their classroom websites or blogs, TED-Ed goes a step further and provides a library of curated lessons that are built around the site's videos. This platform also allows users to take any useful educational video—not just one from the TED website—and easily create a customized lesson around that video. Many of these lessons contain quiz questions and discussion starters, which can be altered to best fit your needs. If you decide to use video as part of a lesson, TED-Ed is one of the best venues for locating existing material, and there is certainly nothing wrong with using something that's already made, especially when you can tweak it to fit your own lesson.

When used appropriately, feature-length movies can serve a similar purpose. According to Rafe Esquith (2007), "The judicious use of film to enrich history is a powerful way for students to learn about the past" (p. 90). Although

Esquith has his students watch entire movies related to the content he teaches, they watch each movie during one after-school session, which is much more effective than monopolizing several class periods. For in-class use—as part of a five-minute teacher's toolkit—short movie clips are useful to engage students in content. For example, appropriate excerpts from films such as *John Adams* or *The Patriot*, used to supplement interactive lessons on the American Revolution, can be more effective than lecturing about the war from a textbook for four weeks and then watching the entire movie over three or four class periods.

Traditional teachers often follow this route: they "teach" through textbook readings, note-taking activities, rote-memory homework assignments, a test, and the movie. During the movie, they'll sit back and grade the tests. Perhaps there might even be a worksheet for students to complete during the movie, which adds a nice sense of control over what is already a disengaging and fruitless endeavor. By contrast, a five-minute teacher uses short, appropriate, and well-timed movie clips as discussion and activity starters. As a result, students become interested in the film's topic and more engaged in the activities that follow naturally. (An added benefit of this approach is that students need not be distracted by "bad" history or irrelevant material. No film is without flaws, particularly those that focus on historical periods.)

Though it is still relatively unknown in the education world, screencasting is one of the most powerful forms of video creation available. Creating a screencast video is also surprisingly easy, even for people who don't consider themselves to be technologically savvy. A simple description of screencasting is when you use an application to capture and record your computer screen. The recorded screen capture is then edited or enhanced with additional audio or video. Most modern computers and laptops come equipped with built-in microphones and webcams, which are all you really need to get started. (To watch a video in which I describe and demonstrate the process of creating a screencast, visit www. learnitin5.com/5-Minute-Teacher-Resources-0.)

To further simplify, imagine you are a math teacher using PowerPoint slides to demonstrate how to solve an equation. With a screencasting application, you could record your voice and narrate the presentation while you use your cursor or drawing tools to walk through and explain the equation. When the screencast is complete, you can upload the final video to a publicly accessible website (such as YouTube or screencast.com) for convenient viewing by your students and—perhaps—their parents. Once the video is hosted on a website, an embed code can easily be generated, and the video can then be placed on a classroom website or blog.

Not only can screencasts be used to ignite remark-able five-minute instruction, they can also become part of a growing web-based archive of brief videos that students can access at any time. These video libraries are amazing resources for both students and parents, and they help the five-minute teacher spend more time providing feedback to and coaching students. How is this so? As your video library becomes an expanding go-to asset, your lesson-planning time is reduced. Indeed, it's possible to produce and post dozens of brief, engaging videos over the course of a single school year or summer. This has the potential to significantly reduce lesson planning for years to come.

If you're eager to dive into video production for your class, you might want to begin with a tool such as Jing. Jing's host site (www.techsmith.com/jing.html) contains many quick video tutorials that will have you screencasting in minutes. Realistically, though, you won't need much tutoring—Jing is remarkably simple. When your screencasting skills advance and you want to produce more aesthetically pleasing videos with better animation and sound (your students will appreciate this), you may want to upgrade to a more powerful tool. Numerous applications exist to meet a variety of needs. Some are free; some are quite costly. Some have just enough bells and whistles to not feel overwhelming; some are for professionals. Once you're ready to produce outstanding videos to engage your students (who, let's be honest, are used to the amazing quality of today's online videos and are fairly difficult to impress), I recommend you research the available options and consider more advanced platforms—you can do much more with them than you can with inferior applications that have fewer editing tools.

Whether you use an existing resource of online videos or your own well-produced screencasts, the role of video in the student-centered classroom cannot be underestimated. Whereas teachers in flipped classrooms encourage the viewing of video lectures as homework, five-minute teachers in student-centered classrooms use video to spark student interest in the activities, lessons, and assignments that follow. Five-minute teachers use brief, engaging videos to place an exclamation mark on their lessons and send students scrambling for further knowledge. (For further information about and examples of video use in classrooms, take advantage of the resources available on www.learnitin5.com/5-Minute-Teacher-Resources-0.)

Become a Guide on the Side

Before I was a teacher, I was a basketball coach. Once I earned my teaching license and moved into the classroom, I brought my coaching skills with me. I organized routine lesson plans and yelled at unprepared students in much the same way as I would shout instructions in the gym during basketball practice. I used to say that coaching made me a better teacher, but the truth was that teaching made me a better coach. The irony is that many years later, I transformed back into a coach—albeit one in a student-centered classroom and not one who hollers instructions to his "players."

How did I get there? After a particularly troubling school year, when I spent most of my days demanding compliance from students who had little interest in completing the stale workbook activities I assigned, I spent time researching motivation and best practices in education—all in an effort to rebuild myself and reflect on learning from my students' perspective. Ultimately, this led to a complete overhaul of my teaching methods and to the creation of the Results Only Learning Environment (Barnes, 2013). When I learned to ignore the illusion of control and eliminate traditional grading methods, I knew I could no longer stand in front of students and lecture for a majority of each class. I also knew that I could no longer dictate exactly how my students would learn. It was imperative to the success of a student-centered classroom that I move to the side and allow my students to become the focal point.

When you transition from teacher to coach, you have to empower students to create their own paths to learning outcomes. You have to point in the right direction and then stay out of their way. This is a unique skill that can take some time to hone, but it's the skill that forms the core of both the student-centered classroom and the five-minute teacher.

The idea of being a "guide on the side" is the most popular notion of this concept of teacher as coach (Smith, 1993), offering and encouraging minimal guidance, shared responsibility, and group collaboration and participation. A five-minute teacher in a student-centered classroom becomes more of a coach than a teacher in the definitive sense—he or she is a member of the group, coordinating and collaborating rather than lecturing and dictating activities and methods of evaluation.

Imagine walking into a gym filled with players eagerly dribbling, shooting, and passing basketballs. Before any organized practice routine begins, the court buzzes with a sort of controlled chaos that resembles a combination of practice and play. Some players stretch, some jog, and others stand around the court discussing the previous night's game. The coach strolls around, chatting with players and calling out casual instructions to individuals about their shooting technique, for example. This informal aspect of the practice—when the coach and players sharpen their craft in a relaxed environment, simultaneously getting comfortable with the skills and strategies associated with the game and building rapport with one another—is as important as the carefully planned regimen that follows.

Now imagine walking into a bustling classroom where some students stand and some sit. Groups of two or three huddle around desks, brainstorming ideas for a group project. Individuals lounge in beanbag chairs reading self-selected books or magazines, while others write in journals or work on laptops or tablets. The teacher is momentarily out of sight as she kneels on the floor in a corner, discussing a book with a reader. A few minutes pass, and the teacher glides to one of the groups and sits in an empty chair, easily fitting in as part of the team. A few questions and a suggestion or two later, and she is off to speak to another student working furiously on an iPad. This constant movement looks (and sometimes sounds) a lot like the controlled chaos of the basketball court. Like the athletes and their coach, these students and their teacher work with a purpose, even if it might not be noticeable to the average onlooker.

As we look back in on the basketball practice, the warm-up period ends and the coach calls the team into a huddle and draws up a new play on a small dry-erase board. He or she explains each step and asks questions to evaluate the players' understanding. Momentarily, the coach becomes a teacher and provides a brief lesson before sending players back to practice what they've just learned. As the players collaborate in small groups, the coach observes and moves gracefully among each group, calling out critical observations and instructions—once again returning to coach mode.

Back in the student-centered classroom, the five-minute teacher moves to a part of the room where she is clearly visible to all students. This is the one place where she always provides instruction, so the students already know that a transition is about to occur. She signals a pause in the action with a clap, a knock-knock joke, or even a song. These simple, but fun, methods for acquiring attention are staples of a seamless student-centered classroom. Once all students have quieted down and found a stopping point, the teacher displays a list of six new subject-related words and phrases on the interactive whiteboard. She instructs the class to write the terms in their journals, with a line in front of each—a precursor to acquiring vocabulary related to the new learning unit.

"Two minutes," she calls. "That's 20 seconds to write each word, and that's a very long time." She runs a clock on the whiteboard for all to see. Rather than add pressure, the timer helps students focus on this interruption of their work, and since they've come to value time, they appreciate every second and work to beat the clock. This is one of many simple techniques a five-minute teacher uses to create habits that make the class successful. These habits do not magically appear; they are coached from the beginning and reinforced constantly. In this case, when the teacher provides two minutes for a simple activity, her students use the clock out of habit. When the bell chimes, the teacher tells her students to consider their understanding of each term. "If you know the word well enough to teach, draw a star on the line next to it. If you've heard of it but can't teach it, draw a check. Finally, if you've never heard the word before today, draw a question mark."

She allows only 30 seconds for this activity, and again the clock ticks. We're about three minutes into this segment of class, and the teacher pauses to poll students on how they've designated each word—a quick formative assessment task that reveals how much time the class might need to master each term. One minute later, she explains that by the end of class, everyone should be able to put a star next to all six terms. "Ready?" she queries. A few students look puzzled, but most know exactly what this means—discovery learning.

The teacher then takes a minute to explain that students can learn the words with any tools at their disposal—books, mobile devices, collaboration, or anything else they can think of, short of asking her for the meanings.

"Remember," she reminds them, "this isn't about memorizing definitions. You have to be able to connect these words and phrases to our unit of study." Seconds later, the familiar chaos ensues, and a quest for knowledge is underway. The teacher moves around the room, back in coach mode. Some students collaborate and share their existing background knowledge. Others look up words on their mobile devices and eagerly share the information they find with peers.

In a similar fashion to the basketball coach during break-out sessions, the five-minute teacher calls out key instructions throughout this activity, reminding students of best research practices, appropriate and safe use of technology, and other previously taught study techniques. For example, she reminds one group of students to look beyond the first page of links in their Google search—a common mistake students make—and asks, "What if you go to the second page of search results? I wonder what you might find there."

The teacher notices a group of students that appears to be finished, so she engages them cheerfully: "So, you have all six, right?" They all nod confidently. "Awesome! Who can teach me the word *invertebrate* and explain how it differs from *vertebrate*?" Two students shrug and begin to read the definitions they wrote in their journals. The teacher gently waves a hand. "Remember," she reminds them, "you have to *teach* the terms, not just recite definitions. What questions need to be asked and answered so you can do that?" Soon, the group members return to their textbooks and computers, looking for pictures, reading about invertebrates and vertebrates, asking one another questions, and finding answers together.

About 20 minutes of collaboration, independent learning, and coaching leads the teacher to believe that most students have the terms mastered. She stands in the familiar spot, and the students begin to settle down.

"Will you please return to your original list?" she asks politely. "Now, revisit each term and see if you can put a star next to it." Again, she polls the class. "How many of you have six stars?" She observes carefully and notes on her class roster that four students' hands are at their sides. "How many of you have at least five stars?" All hands go up. This quick evaluation is critical, since it tells her who still needs help to reach mastery. She explains that they will begin the next day with some peer teaching; students will share the methods they used to learn the new vocabulary while teaching the terms to one another.

In the few minutes that are left, students read or work on unrelated projects. In a student-centered, results-only classroom, students are constantly engaged in some sort of ongoing (perhaps yearlong) project that helps them demonstrate mastery of a wide variety of learning outcomes. Some days, they spend most of class on these, but whenever they finish an activity early, they immediately return to their yearlong projects. This is yet another habit that a five-minute teacher instills from the beginning of the year. The teacher uses this time to quietly approach each of the four students who didn't star all six terms. She asks about their strategies and offers some tips to improve their discovery process in the future. Finally, she assures them that they'll be ready to teach the words before the end of the next class.

This is how a five-minute teacher operates—by coaching students to discover new concepts on their own. He or she understands how to use "warm-up" time effectively to emphasize technique and build rapport. Classes are organized with plenty of transitions between activities. During breakout sessions—when individuals or small groups work on their skills and discover new content—a five-minute teacher knows when to stay on the sidelines, quiet and out of the way, and when to coach, using student-centered strategies that elicit learning and don't give too much information away.

Just as an astute coach realizes that his or her players will learn faster if the plays are explained as they run them, a five-minute teacher understands that well-placed (and well-timed) questions create natural conversations that lead to authentic learning. This combination of brief segments of instruction followed by collaboration and discovery creates a marvelous student-centered learning environment. Facilitating it all is a five-minute teacher who, to the casual observer, often looks like an athletic coach. In the end, both are winners, and so are their players.

The previous example showed a five-minute teacher facilitating a lesson in which she abandoned the old-school stand-and-deliver method in favor of coaching strategies. This lesson's success is built on the following strategies. When planning any lesson, some or all of these should be part of it.

Use a timer. A clearly visible timer motivates students to remain task-oriented. It's best to keep activities brief. If you need 20 or more minutes for an activity, try to break it into several shorter sessions, setting the clock to a specific time for each. If possible, set the timer to a fun sound that ends the activity and signals transition to something new; this way, students learn that the completion of a brief task is a pleasurable experience.

Ask "What if?" Rather than simply answering questions or guiding students to knowledge, help them learn how to find their own answers. Students will discover concepts and skills more readily when they are given the chance to seek knowledge independently. Beginning questions with "What if. . . ?" is an excellent way to spark further investigation.

Supply multiple paths to learning. Traditional teachers have been conditioned to use workbooks, worksheets, homework, and textbook questions, but there are far better alternatives. When planning lessons and projects, consider various paths to the learning outcome. Use web tools, mobile apps, arts and crafts, manipulatives, reflection, and small-group activities instead of traditional methods to provoke a quest for knowledge.

Designate a "pause-for-instruction" spot. Coach students from the beginning that independent or collaborative learning is sometimes interrupted for whole-group instruction or a transition to a different discovery activity. If you consistently deliver that instruction from one spot in the room, students will become accustomed to it and learn to pause their work when they see you standing there.

Be mobile. When your students are constantly transitioning from one activity to the next, you have to be on the go. Although you want students to become independent learners, it's important for them to know that you are a part of their never-ending search for knowledge. Therefore, you must move around the room frequently, talking to individual students and groups as often as possible. Sometimes, just gliding past students and saying "That's interesting" or "Think about sharing that with the class" is enough to remind them that you are part of the learning process.

Become invisible. There are times when getting out of the way is as important as instructing and answering questions. As the school year progresses, students will become more independent and less reliant on you (but only if they see you less). Find things to do in the classroom that reassure them that you're present but remind them that they need to learn on their own. When my students become excellent independent learners, I often stand by the door (sometimes I even walk into the hallway, completely out of sight). This disappearing act may last no more than 30 to 40 seconds, but it instills confidence in students that they are part of a learning community and can function without the teacher.

Help Students Become Independent Learners

You may have gleaned from previous examples that collaboration is essential to the success of a five-minute teacher. Traditional teachers often consider collaboration to be nothing more than students working in groups of three or four to solve a math problem or complete a science lab. With this mindset and in this environment, students usually return to rows of desks and individual seatwork as soon the assignment is complete. This kind of group work is the most basic type of cooperative learning, and it has a place in a successful classroom. However, it is typically about completing one task, whereas the collaboration that happens in a student-centered classroom is ongoing and—in many cases—not about a single activity. In a student-centered learning environment, collaboration fans intrinsic motivation and creates independent learners because students have greater control over their own learning.

Consider the aforementioned vocabulary acquisition activity. A traditional cooperative learning approach might be to place the six terms on a worksheet and provide students with textbooks or other resources. The directions would likely instruct students to look up the definitions; the teacher might even stretch the activity by encouraging students to discuss the terms and use them in sentences. In this scenario, are the students working together? It's debatable. Although they are grouped together, students will more than likely divide up the work and then copy from one another. There's not much higher-level thinking going on here.

By contrast, a five-minute teacher creates a less structured—though much more effective and fun—lesson, asking students to learn the terms using any method they choose. This collaborative activity is fueled by intrinsic motivation. Whereas many students in the traditional group activity might hesitate to look up words and write definitions, those in a student-centered classroom are eager to learn and often choose to use mobile devices, books, and background knowledge. They regard the assignment as a quest for knowledge, and they decide what that quest looks like for themselves.

An important aspect of being a five-minute teacher and creating a student-centered classroom is the willingness to promote autonomy among students. Within collaborative projects, such autonomy can manifest when students are given options to demonstrate their learning and the ability to choose their own partners—something many teachers are often reluctant to do. However, it's difficult to promote autonomy when students are constantly told exactly what to do and with whom to do it. When students have the freedom to choose their partners, it's much easier for them to feel like true members of a team and agree on what the final product of the assignment will look like.

The common perception of allowing students to construct their groups is that they will not work because students only want to spend time with their friends. For students who have not spent much time in a results-only classroom with a five-minute teacher, this may be true. In fact, one poor project may be necessary for these students to learn how to work efficiently, whether they're with friends or not. It is important to allow students to fail, as long as proper feedback about their failure is provided and a lesson is learned. Throughout my career as a five-minute teacher, I've seen plenty of students fail one project only to tell me that they didn't put enough thought into choosing their partners. It's nice to see these students change their approach and then flourish—an invaluable lesson they'd never learn if their groups were determined for them.

Autonomy doesn't end at choosing partners. For example, if you want students to demonstrate an understanding of proper research strategies, including evaluating and citing sources, then allow them to choose virtually any subject to research. Many traditional teachers assign topics from a pre-approved list. Though they may believe (as I once did) that it's better to evaluate the same idea over and over, I found this approach to be short-sighted as my students became less interested in the project and topic. A five-minute teacher allows students to choose their topics, their partners, and which digital tools they want to use to research and deliver the information. In my own classes, I cover the research process explicitly through a combination of direct instruction and collaborative activities. The rest of the process is done through coaching and self-discovery. What used to be arduous when I taught traditionally transformed into something exciting for both my students and me.

Best of all, it's easy to structure collaborative projects in any subject. An elementary math teacher can have students create a project that requires them to explore various applications for fractions in the real world. High school students learning about DNA could be given the option of studying forensic science. They could create simulations, using the technology of their choice, and compare real-life forensic science to its portrayal on popular television shows. Instead of telling middle school students that they have to learn about ancient Greece, imagine if the teacher asked groups to choose any civilization from a list. Students would engage in group discussions about the evolution of various cultures and the events that affected their progress. Through various methods, they could then compare different civilizations and how they evolved. Choices such as these put students in charge and create the autonomy that is crucial to the success of a student-centered classroom that is based on results rather than the path to learning. In addition, creative, in-depth projects that are driven by student choice inspire independent, genuine learning for learning's sake, and there's nothing more amazing than this in education.

Develop a Toolkit of Student-Driven Activities

Consider the following scenario. A middle school student—Jackson—is seated at a computer and is reviewing content from three websites, each open in a separate browser window. He's logged on to an education version of the poster application Glogster, he's using the video creation tool Animoto, and he's looking at cartoon avatars on the podcasting site Voki. His teacher approaches quietly, trying not to break his intense concentration, and asks, "So, what are you thinking?"

Eyes still focused on the computer screen, Jackson explains that he is using Animoto to produce a 30-second video about the novel he just finished, which was part of an independent reading project. The video will contain graphic representations of the book and its main characters, along with brief slides that introduce the book's title, author, and setting. He's also creating a 60-second Voki podcast in which he will narrate a summary of the story and a brief review of the book. The teacher inquires about the role of Glogster, and

Jackson quickly says that he will embed both the podcast and the video into a Glogster poster, which he'll then share on the class website. After some brief words of encouragement, the teacher then moves on to a nearby student to answer questions about a web tool she is using on the same project.

To develop this kind of independent learning, the classroom must be filled with student-driven activities. For students to drive the learning process, though, it's important to have a wealth of resources from which they can choose. This is no small task. Indeed, there are numerous barriers to building a toolkit of student-driven activities and resources, not the least of which is understanding how to locate or create these tools and how to teach effective and appropriate technology use.

As Jackson demonstrates, students become engaged in student-driven activities because they are afforded the freedom and opportunity to demonstrate what they've learned in a variety of ways. The key to Jackson's success is an intimate knowledge of the digital tools with which he'll deliver the information. Although today's students, especially teenagers, are comfortable with the Internet and social media, we can't assume that they're immediately knowledgeable of the applications available for teaching and learning. Even though the digital tools mentioned in the previous example are relatively easy to use, proper application to learning must still be taught. Of course, this means the teacher must first know how to use the tools.

The best approach to developing a toolkit of applications and activities that is uniquely suited to the five-minute teacher is to spend as much time as possible learning about the tools available and then teaching them to your students often. If you introduce a new program or application several times a month, then your toolkit will quickly be well stocked. When it's time to share a new concept or discuss a new topic, students are able to choose which tools best fit their needs. You don't need to be an expert on all devices and apps, but having a general understanding of them will make you a more effective teacher. For example, a number of learning sites offer powerful tools for formative assessment and can be used on a computer or mobile device. Imagine telling your students that you want them to use their cell phones to text in class (to respond to a questionnaire). They'll love it, and you'll gather key information about learning in seconds. With a little practice and some high-quality how-to videos, it's possible to master some of these applications in an evening and integrate them into your class the next day.

Keep in mind that almost any hardware, software, or web application can be part of a five-minute teacher's technology toolkit. Slides on an interactive whiteboard, manipulatives, and handheld devices all offer excellent means for enhancing direct instruction. Rather than showing students a weather formation with static pictures, the intuitive five-minute science teacher invites his or her students to learn about and locate weather systems by searching for them on a tablet or other handheld device. Students then share links to this information on a class wiki or web-based post-it wall (e.g., www.padlet.com).

Virtually any resource can be a smart addition to a five-minute teacher's tech toolkit, as long as instruction is carefully woven into what students do with the particular tool. Too often, the traditional teacher gives verbal instructions that consume five minutes or more of class time. Students are naturally eager to move—to do something—and time spent sitting still and disengaged diminishes this enthusiasm. Rather than lecture, get to your toolkit early and often, and watch your student-centered classroom erupt into learning. (Once again, check out the toolkit resources at www.learnitin5.com/5-Minute-Teacher-Resources-0.)

The following brief list of tools is a great digital foundation for any five-minute teacher. It begins with a classroom website, as this should be the hub that houses many of the teacher's presentations and much of the students' work. In addition, several of the tools mentioned have mobile apps, making them even more accessible.

Wiki Classroom Website. *Potential hosts:* EditMe, PBworks, Wikispaces. Some of these are free with space limits, and others have monthly fees. *Uses:* A wiki classroom site can serve as a home base for activities, unit plans, calendars, attachments, instructions, and private student workspaces.

Classroom Blog. *Potential hosts:* Kidblog, Blogger, Edublogs, Wordpress. Some of these are designed specifically for education, whereas others are not but offer more functionality. *Uses:* Teachers in any subject and at virtually any grade level can make excellent use of class blogs. A blog gives students a place to create and curate information on any topic. With the Common Core State Standards emphasizing writing across the curriculum, student blogs should be an essential, integrated aspect of all classrooms.

Presentation Sites. *Potential sites and applications:* Animoto, Magisto, Slideshare, Keynote, Techsmith (which hosts Jing, Snagit, and Camtasia Studio). Each functions somewhat differently, so you'll want to explore which ones best fit your classroom. *Uses:* Teachers can create amazing presentations and screencasts that beautifully supplement any lesson. In addition, students love the interactivity of these tools for presenting information to their peers.

Social Media. *Potential applications:* Twitter, Flipboard, Instagram, Edmodo, Schoology, Scoop.it! Some social media sites are designed specifically for education, giving them the privacy features that administrators covet. However, the trade-off is that they lack some of the accessibility that other sites provide. If your school blocks social media completely, check out those that target education exclusively. Regardless of which sites you use, it's imperative to teach acceptable use to your students throughout the year. Sites such as Twitter can be amazing communication and curation tools, but students need to be well aware of the associated dangers. *Uses:* Social media is here to stay. Students love it, so why not embrace it as the powerful teaching and learning tool that it can be? For example, create a Twitter hashtag for your class. Allow your students to tweet their comments, and share the hashtag conversation on your interactive whiteboard. You'll be amazed at the results.

Tools That Promote Thinking. *Potential resources:* MAX Teaching strategies (Forget, 2004), AVID strategies

(Crain, Mullen, & Swanson, 2002), *Essential Questions* (McTighe & Wiggins, 2013), *Learning Targets* (Moss & Brookhart, 2012). These remarkable resources give teachers go-to strategies that engage students and promote critical thinking during student-centered activities. *Uses:* Create effective questions to stimulate small-group conversation. Differentiate instruction with targeted outcomes for various learning styles. Teach students to be active readers who travel beyond the surface of difficult text.

Conclusion

My first year teaching in a student-centered Results Only Learning Environment concluded with performance reviews—written narratives that evaluate yearlong student performance. It had been an amazing nine months in which I rebuilt myself as a teacher, and my students experienced the kind of autonomy they'd never seen before in any class. Before mailing the reports home, I wanted each of my students to read his or her report and have an opportunity to discuss it with me.

One student asked me why all teachers didn't have the sort of student-centered classroom that I had. He enjoyed the freedoms, choices, and collaboration that the results-only classroom provided him. I explained that many teachers weren't yet ready to let go of the control they thought they had over their classes. They only knew one way to teach, but it was up to us to change this thinking by talking about how we learn best.

Years later, I'm thrilled to see that many teachers are now joining the movement and creating exciting student-centered classrooms. My own colleagues are cutting back homework assignments, using amazing interactive teaching and learning strategies, creating engaging yearlong projects, and using technology like never before. The product of this creativity is a workshop-like classroom that puts students at the center of the action and moves the teacher to the side. Traditional educators are quickly becoming five-minute teachers and transforming education as we know it. How about it? Are you ready to join this amazing movement and become a five-minute teacher?

Acknowledgments

Some time ago, a collection of brilliant minds at ASCD hatched a very cool plan to publish short-form books. "What if teachers could read a book at home one night, and apply what they learn in the classroom the next day?" they wondered. ASCD Arias was born, and I was asked to be part of the launch. I can't say enough about the faith these people have placed in me to be part of their brainchild. All I can do is offer my heartfelt thanks to these ASCD superstars who churn out one awesome book after another. Please allow me to shout thank you to Stefani Roth and Laura Lawson, two of the smartest people I know, who for some unknown reason have expressed their confidence in my abilities. I'm not worthy. Thanks to Jamie Greene, who valiantly faces the challenge of cleaning up my messy drafts and makes me look better than I am. Thanks to Genny Ostertag for added support. Thank you Julia Liapidova and Marissa Bialecki for your tireless efforts in promoting my work. And a huge thanks to Richard Papale for making my role in this project a reality.

As always, thanks to Mollie, my amazing wife and the compass that keeps me on track.

To give your feedback on this publication and be entered into a drawing for a free ASCD Arias e-book, click here or type in this web location: **www.ascd.org/ariasfeedback**

ENCORE

THE 5-MINUTE TEACHER

Following are some frequently asked questions about how to maintain a student-centered classroom as a five-minute teacher, along with some suggestions.

FREQUENTLY ASKED QUESTIONS

Q I've taught for 25 years with lectures and worksheets. What is the easiest way for an old-school teacher like me to become a five-minute teacher?

A First, know that if you're asking, you're already on your way. The most difficult part of my own transition was realizing that I needed to change. Second, know that it's a difficult road that requires perseverance. Third, use the specific five-minute teacher strategies outlined here. If you talk less and get your students moving, you'll be well on your way.

Q What if I ask students to work on computers or mobile devices, and they end up playing games or surfing the web?

A You have to coach independent learning constantly. Remember, your students are kids, and they'll make mistakes. Be sure the activities and projects you ask them to do are engaging and create plenty of choice, so students will want to work rather than play.

Q What about those students who gravitate toward games or social media, no matter what I do?

A There will always be students who struggle to see value in the learning opportunities you provide. One thing I've had great success with is what I call a "tech timeout." This doesn't mean you should stop using technology; it means you should take a timeout from academics and use technology strictly for fun—as long as students stick to guidelines for appropriate use. I even allow the use of social media during these tech timeouts. The standard guidelines are that students are not allowed to post to social media sites and they're not allowed to text. As long as the websites they visit are appropriate, pretty much anything else goes during this time. When they recognize the "reward" of relative free time with their devices or on their favorite websites, reluctant learners have more incentive to complete class activities and projects.

Q How can I ensure appropriate use of mobile devices in my classroom?

A All mobile devices should be on tabletops and desktops, in full view, from the moment students enter the room. If a device is on a student's lap, then the activity is very likely inappropriate. Don't hesitate to teach students about the dangers of Internet predators, along with the harm that can be done by hurtful posts about peers (cyber bullying). There is no need to shield even your youngest students from the potential dangers of the Internet and social media. Importantly, be sure to involve parents in this necessary aspect of education. I find that when children understand the risks involved with social media use, they tend to err on the side of caution.

Q I have reluctant learners who don't usually work well in groups. Should I isolate them?

A Removing a reluctant learner from collaborative activities should be a last resort and done only after a serious conversation with the student about the benefits of your learning community. I have found that involving at-risk students in groups typically brings out the best in them, especially if the other students are coached to do all they can to encourage participation from all group members. Often, asking a reluctant learner to take on a leadership role sparks interest in cooperative learning.

Q I'm not a technology teacher; how am I supposed to integrate all of these web tools?

A First, realize that you probably know more than you think. Use resources that are already available to help you use and teach various web tools. For instance, I learned screencasting at a technology conference, and then I followed up this introduction by watching many how-to videos and reading teacher blogs on the subject. Once you educate yourself, practice often. Finally, rely on your students to become experts. You'll find that they quickly will.

Q Without the use of objective materials like worksheets, tests, and quizzes, how can I be sure my students are learning?

A Observation is a five-minute teacher's best method of evaluation. You will notice amazing growth points daily, weekly, and monthly, simply by observing how your students apply concepts from your minilessons to their project work. If you create an engaging yearlong project that involves the use of many learning outcomes, you'll witness phenomenal growth over a nine-month period. Be confident in yourself as an evaluator; like your students, you'll improve over time.

References

Barnes, M. (2013). *Role reversal: Achieving uncommonly excellent results in the student-centered classroom.* Alexandria, VA: ASCD.

Crain, H., Mullen, M., & Swanson, M. C. (2002). *Advancement via individual determination: The write path English language arts teacher guide.* San Diego, CA: AVID Center.

Esquith, R. (2007). *Teach like your hair's on fire: The methods and madness inside room 56.* New York: Penguin.

Forget, M. A. (2004). *MAX teaching with reading and writing: Classroom activities for helping students learn new subject matter while acquiring literacy skills.* Portsmouth, VA: Trafford.

McTighe, J., & Wiggins, G. (2013). *Essential questions: Opening doors to student understanding.* Alexandria, VA: ASCD.

Moss, C., & Brookhart, S. M. (2012). *Learning targets: Helping students aim for understanding in today's lesson.* Alexandria, VA: ASCD.

Ong, R. (2004). The role of reflection in student learning: A study of its effectiveness in complementing PBL environment. Paper presented at the PBL 2004 Conference, Cancún, Mexico.

Smith, K. (1993, October). Becoming the guide on the side. *Educational Leadership, 51*(2), 35–37. Retrieved from http://www.ascd.org/publications/educational-leadership/oct93/vol51/num02/Becoming-the-"Guide-on-the-Side".aspx

Related Resources

At the time of publication, the following ASCD resources were available (ASCD stock numbers appear in parentheses). For up-to-date information about ASCD resources, go to www.ascd.org. You can search the complete archives of Educational Leadership at http://www.ascd.org/el.

ASCD EDge®
Exchange ideas and connect with other educators interested in student-centered classrooms on the social networking site ASCD EDge at http://ascdedge.ascd.org/

Print Products
Assignments Matter: Making the Connections That Help Students Meet Standards by Eleanor Dougherty (#112048)
Inspiring the Best in Students by Jonathan C. Erwin (#110006)
Learning for Keeps: Teaching the Strategies Essential for Creating Independent Learners by Rhoda Koenig (#111003)
Productive Group Work: How to Engage Students, Build Teamwork, and Promote Understanding by Nancy Frey, Douglas Fisher, and Sandi Everlove (#109018)
Role Reversal: Achieving Uncommonly Excellent Results in the Student-Centered Classroom by Mark Barnes (#113004)
Total Participation Techniques: Making Every Student an Active Learner by Pérsida Himmele and William Himmele (#111037)

ASCD PD Online® Courses
Project-Based Learning and the Common Core Standards (#PD13OC008)
Understanding Student Motivation, 2nd Edition (#PD11OC106)

For more information: send e-mail to member@ascd.org; call 1-800-933-2723 or 703-578-9600, press 2; send a fax to 703-575-5400; or write to Information Services, ASCD, 1703 N. Beauregard St., Alexandria, VA 22311-1714 USA.

About the Author

Mark Barnes is a veteran classroom teacher, education consultant, and author of the critically acclaimed ASCD book *Role Reversal: Achieving Uncommonly Excellent Results in the Student-Centered Classroom.* He is also a champion for student-centered classrooms and the Results Only Learning Environment.

WHAT KEEPS YOU UP AT NIGHT?

ASCD Arias begin with a burning question and then provide the answers you need today—in a convenient format you can read in one sitting and immediately put into practice. Available in both print and digital editions.

Answers You Need
from Voices You Trust

ASCD | arias™